ISBN# 1-56245-045-X

Great Quotations Publishing Inc.
1967 Quincy Court
Glendale Heights, IL 60139
Printed in Hong Kong

Y0-BNF-601

Parents and students have submitted written tributes to teacher honorees. A sampling of these tributes are contained in this special calendar honoring teachers who are offering those special "Gifts of Time," those who go the extra mile for their students.

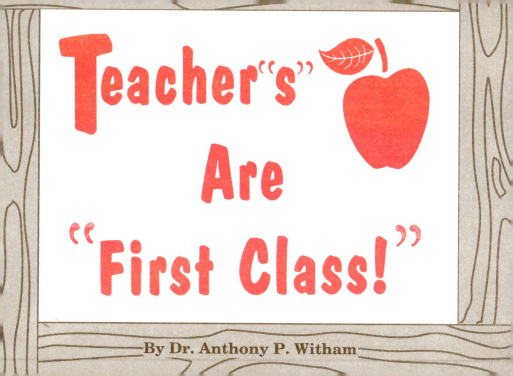

Phone Numbers

Other Calendars by Great Quotations

Apple A Day
Each Day A New Beginning
Friend Forever
Golf Forever ... Work Whenever
Home Is Where The Heart Is
Seasonings

Simple Ways To Say I Love You
To A Very Special Dad
To A Very Special Mon
Teachers Are "First Class!"

Other Books by Great Quotations

A Light Heart Lives Long
Better Place.
Food For Thought
Golden Years, Golden Words
Heal The World - Make It A
Hollywords
Reflections
Sports Page
Women on Men

Ancient Echoes
Birthday Wishes
Don't Marry, Be Happy
Great Quotes Great Comedians
Harvest Of Thoughts
Love Streams
The Best Of Business Humor
To A Very Special Husband
Who Really Said
Works of Heart

Teachers who bring good feelings to children can never fully measure their influence on the life of a child. As you begin a new year, may you continue in your positive and caring ways.

January 1

Think of all the children yet to feel special to someone and be reminded of how much caring teachers are needed! Have a safe and Happy New Year.

December 31

"Every now and then, I peek into the classroom. She can correct a child's errors and raise self-esteem simultaneously. Her love for the children shows through."

Parent Tribute

January 2

"The door to the human heart can be opened only from the inside. No amount of coursework can assure a positive and caring attitude in a teacher."

AFI Notable Quote

December 30

"My daughter's teacher isn't shy to tell students how proud he is of them when they make good efforts. My daughter has been deeply touched by his many kindnesses."

Parent Tribute

January 3

The surest way to knock a chip off a pupil's shoulder is with a pat on the back.

December 29

Accept the individuality of each student when others prepare for uniform responses.

January 4

"To see the world through children's eyes, a teacher needs infinite emotional flexibility."

AFI Notable Quote

December 28

"One day in art class, my teacher noticed I was feeling bad. He sat down and took the time to listen to my problems. He made me feel so much better. He's a great teacher and a greater friend."

Student Tribute

January 5

"She will tutor us on her own time when needed. She inspired me in a way no other teacher has. I watched her teach and I got the message that education can be fun and rewarding as well as fulfilling."

Student Tribute

$2 + \frac{1}{3}$

December 27

"My child's teacher has that caring attitude which encourages children to try their best without intimidating them. She's a role model for both of us."

Parent Tribute

January 6

"As a teacher, the greatest possible good I can do for my students is not to share my talents with them, but to help them discover and use their own."

AFI Notable Quote

December 26

Believe that each student has potential for some success when others neglect to nurture possibilities.

January 7

just for a moment to see you as I do;
then, maybe, finally, you would see
for yourself this beautiful teacher
who matters so much to all who have
had the privilege of sharing your
enthusiasm for learning, for life!"

Student Tribute

December 25

"My child's teacher attended a ceremony at which my son received a scouting award. He will never forget that act of caring or the super teacher who really enjoys her job."

Parent Tribute

January 8

"She has a magic in her voice that children respond to. My daughter has grown so much under her guidance. A gift from God."

Parent Tribute

December 24

"My teacher helps students with problems after school and during free periods. She helped me cope with family problems when my father lost his job. My teacher always has a positive attitude which brings smiles to the kids."

Student Tribute

January 9

"As a parent of a teenager, I have relied on her as my touchstone and stabilizer. She took my daughter with average ability to new heights of achievement and personal fulfillment."

Parent Tribute

December 23

Compliment the smallest efforts of students when others overlook opportunities for praise.

January 10

Am I prepared today with words of good cheer for my students; to bring smiles, to banish tears?

December 22

"She goes that extra mile to call parents at home on her time to resolve special concerns. She teaches important values and attitudes that students can learn from."

Parent Tribute

January 11

"Our teacher introduced us to ourselves. We learned who we were and what we wanted to be. We were no longer strangers to ourselves."

Student Tribute

December 21

"He donates awesome amounts of time to promote music appreciation and always finds the time to be a friend to his students. Truly an admirable man."

Parent Tribute

January 12

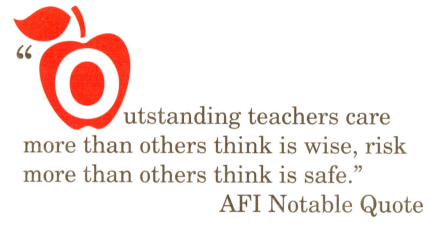

"Outstanding teachers care more than others think is wise, risk more than others think is safe."

AFI Notable Quote

December 20

Demand only the best efforts from each student when others overlook opportunities for praise.

January 13

"I used to get horrible grades until she woke me up to myself and my potential. Her belief in me has raised my grades and self-esteem. It feels so wonderful to hear her compliment my grades in Spanish II."

Student Tribute

December 19

"My teacher has inspired me to be the best carpenter I can be. He only accepts quality work. His positive attitude even on the worst of days is simply amazing."

Student Tribute

January 14

"She made such an impression on my child that he was considering failing so he could repeat second grade with his hero and best friend."

Parent Tribute

December 18

"She has an enthusiasm for science and encourages children in innovative projects that enrich the mind. From the outer reaches of the heavens to the inner core of mother earth, the children explore the universe."

Parent Tribute

January 15

"We are the real heroes of everyday. We come up each morning to shine brightly on children that embrace and need us."

AFI Notable Quote

December 17

Exhibit a passion for learning and for your subject when others show too little enthusiasm.

January 16

"My teacher arrives early each day to provide tutoring and will help anyone during her free period. She never turns us down or away if we need help and never makes us feel dumb."

Student Tribute

December 16

"She has helped my daughter in so many ways. I have seen my child mature so much this past year. This teacher doesn't pressure kids to learn but provides opportunities for individual growth."

Parent Tribute

January 17

"This teacher inspired my daughter to have greater self-confidence in herself at a time when she had none. She mixed praise with extra help and discipline as needed."

Parent Tribute

December 15

"My daughter struggled through school and barely achieved mainly with help at home. Her teacher then helped her develop study skills which have moved her grades to A's and B's."

Parent Tribute

January 18

Write some encouraging and happy notes to students today. Written encouragement packs more power than verbal encouragement. It can be read over and over.

December 14

Forgive and forget classroom misconduct once resolved when others carry grudges with students.

January 19

"I have had my dad as a teacher, track coach and youth group leader. Every day that goes by I admire him a little more for inspiring the best in me."

Student Tribute

December 13

"We thank you Mrs. B. for always making yourself available to us when we have those difficult decisions and moments. We thank you for your extra effort and concern for us."

Parent Tribute

January 20

"The one teacher that stands out in my mind always gave me the five or ten minutes when he saw me struggling. He complimented me when I deserved it."

Student Tribute

December 12

"I'm convinced that if she was not the compassionate and competent teacher she is, my son would not have survived a family crisis as well as he did AND continue achieving at school."

Parent Tribute

January 21

"No one should demand that teachers pretend perfection; only that they remain willing to grow."

AFI Notable Quote

December 11

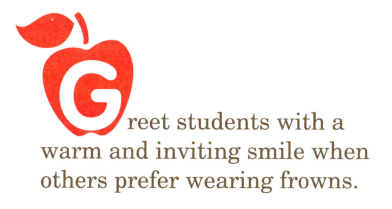

Greet students with a warm and inviting smile when others prefer wearing frowns.

January 22

"My son is excited about going to school and feels that way when he comes home! It means so much to parents to have such a teacher influencing a child."

Parent Tribute

December 10

"I have been having family problems and live in a foster home. My teacher told me if I needed help or someone to talk with she would always be there. No one else ever told me that before."

Student Tribute

January 23

"An exceptional teacher who doesn't worry about how much time and energy it takes to get the job done. He has made the difference in reviving my son's interest in school."

Parent Tribute

December 9

"My son had much difficulty last year partially due to a hearing loss. He lagged far behind in his assignments. His teacher reversed this trend and brought out his best. He now loves school and his new found feelings of self-worth."

Parent Tribute

January 24

Remember, students love to hear stories about yourself. A well-told story can be like a sunbeam in a sick room.

December 8

Help students discover their special gifts when others overlook hidden talents.

January 25

"She repeatedly does acts of kindness, rewards her students by taking a few out to dinner if they have reached their goals, sends birthday cards, and takes time to listen."

Parent Tribute

December 7

"She's the epitome of excellence in teaching. She gives endlessly to each child in need. Children come away with feelings of self-worth, self-confidence and self-awareness: a one-of-a-kind teacher!"

Parent Tribute

January 26

"Work papers are filled with personal encouragement. The mood is always upbeat. She let the sunshine into my daughter's life."

Parent Tribute

December 6

"He has a special way of making students feel special. I've seen him stop a shy child on a class trip, say something kind or funny, and the smile on the child's face was priceless."

Parent Tribute

January 27

"They are truly great teachers who can deal with us when we aren't up to par, and can still appreciate us just exactly as we are."

AFI Notable Quote

December 5

Inspire a passion for lifetime learning in students when others limit themselves to mastering a lesson plan.

January 28

"She really helps me. She tutored me this summer and has made this my best year of school. My first report card had C's and above. I felt so proud when I got it."

Student Tribute

December 4

"My teacher makes our class come alive! I have retained more from her class than any other. She made our Anthropology I class an exciting experience where everyone had to contribute."

Student Tribute

January 29

"She definitely goes the extra mile for her students. She encourages creative writing skills by 'publishing' books that encourage lifetime readers. She is truly appreciated by everyone."

Parent Tribute

December 3

"He is a magical kind of teacher who brings subject matter to life. His enthusiasm and teaching style makes learning an unexpected and intriguing experience."

Student Tribute

January 30

"It's because of teachers who know us, those who seem to understand, that we find the going easy when we need a helping hand."

AFI Notable Quote

December 2

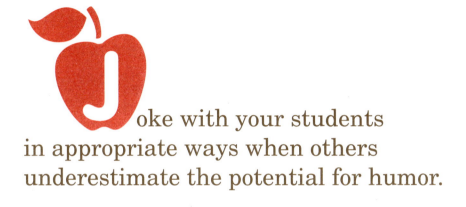

Joke with your students in appropriate ways when others underestimate the potential for humor.

January 31

"She first touched my life by giving me piano lessons when I was seven. Her teaching style, encouragement and personal touch have made a remarkable difference in my life."

Student Tribute

December 1

"Every child wants to learn in his class not to get a good grade, but to enjoy the good feelings that accompany contributing something worthwhile."

Parent Tribute

February 1

"Her influence on fourth and fifth graders at our school has been remarkable. She provides positive reinforcement to the point where every child is made to feel special."

Parent Tribute

November 30

"In the time she has been with us as an art teacher, she has endeared herself to students and staff. She has touched and nurtured the creative instincts of her pupils and has expanded their potential."

Parent Tribute

February 2

Teachers discover that love for the profession and pupils can bring the greatest joy to the most unpleasant tasks.

November 29

Know the name and something special about each student when others fail to make students feel valued.

February 3

"She has that special gift of instilling self-esteem in each child. She sacrifices much of her own time to provide opportunities for each child to experience some success."

Parent Tribute

November 28

"She's a great technician and goes that extra mile to help us understand. I'm a slow learner but she treats me like a quick learner."

Student Tribute

February 4

"She has been more than a teacher to us. There's more warmth and friendliness in her class than in any I've ever been in. She never once said, 'I don't have time for you'!"

Student Tribute

November 27

"If we have personal problems that are affecting our learning, she's quick to notice and offer an attentive ear and sound advice."

Student Tribute

February 5

The student who needs your guidance and support the most is probably the one who has given his least in your class.

November 26

Laugh at yourself and be real before your students when others take themselves too seriously.

February 6

"She is an example of patience and perseverance. She demonstrates great qualities of kindness and enthusiasm. My daughter has developed this year in a very positive way thanks to this great teacher."

Parent Tribute

November 25

"When my son had problems, she responded with extra attention, time, phone calls, and helpful advice on how to guide activities at home to increase possibilities for success at school."

Parent Tribute

February 7

"He has been a positive influence on my son's life, he makes himself available at any time. He has encouraged, advised, enforced and taught my son in decision-making. We are so grateful."

Parent Tribute

November 24

"My daughter said, 'She brings glory to the name of teacher,' and for good reason. Her caring ways have saved both the lives and self-respect of so many students: a real treasure."

Parent Tribute

February 8

I am reminded that as I generate positive attitudes in my classroom I can create a chain reaction of positive thoughts and ideas.

November 23

Model compassion in resolving difficulties students may face when others appear preoccupied with perfection.

February 9

"She's the role model for teachers who care about resolving special needs of students. She gives of herself selflessly and untiringly. An inspiration to her colleagues."

Parent Tribute

November 22

"My daughter is very comfortable with her and has a desire to work hard and do her best. She creates special activities for students as rewards. My child looks forward to school."

Parent Tribute

February 10

"She helped save my academic career from ruin. My grades were bad and she sat me down and gave me the lecture of my life. It turned me around. I'm earning A's. I'm forever in debt to her."

Student Tribute

November 21

"My daughter has a learning disability and this fine teacher gives her the endless patience and attention she requires. My daughter's attitude has made a complete reversal."

Parent Tribute

February 11

"**A** happy classroom is not one without problems or disappointments, but one that handles them with understanding and love."

AFI Notable Quote

November 20

Nurture habits of reading and study in your students when others focus more on completing texts and tests.

February 12

"Our child was filled with anxiety about going to first grade until he met his teacher. She has given him good feelings, self-control and self-confidence. We are eternally grateful."
Parent Tribute

November 19

"My teacher does extra things enthusiastically and everyone around him cannot help but get swept up in the excitement. He leaves students feeling better about themselves."

Student Tribute

February 13

"She refused to accept my daughter's self-doubt and helped rebuild her belief in herself to the point of making the honor roll."

Parent Tribute

November 18

Valentine hugs to all caring teachers, those who are making this world a little bit better for our children and families. We applaud your special efforts.

February 14

"**F**or ignoring the possibility of the fool in me, and laying hold of the possibility of good—I'm forever grateful."

AFI Notable Quote

November 17

"It isn't very often you get an uncle for a teacher. He's fun and doesn't show favoritism. It's nice to know someone who cares so much about his students, someone you can talk to."

Student Tribute

February 15

"She teaches my daughter things that I try to teach her with little success. Even when she's sick, she wants to go to school! Now that's quite a tribute to her teacher!"

Parent Tribute

November 16

Observe and report symptoms of distress in students when others may overlook the value of early intervention.

February 16

"She always goes above and beyond what's expected of her. My son brings home a positive attitude and lots of useful activities. He looks forward to school each day as the best event of the day."

Parent Tribute

November 15

"She is a very special teacher who is willing to take her free period to talk to a student in need. Her positive attitude attracts people and inspires achievement."

Parent Tribute

February 17

"The days that your students are made happy are the days that make your students wise."

AFI Notable Quote

November 14

"He finds the time to listen and to encourage us when we're uncertain or down. His class is challenging and exciting."

Student Tribute

February 18

"My daughter is hearing impaired
and mainstreamed. Her teacher keeps
in constant touch by phone and sends
home helpful progress reports,
suggestions, etc. She has been
a real blessing to us."

Parent Tribute

November 13

Prepare lesson plans which offer each student some opportunities for success when others plan for a uniform response.

February 19

"She was my art teacher. Never did I learn so much. She also became my best friend, encouraging me always to be my best and to discover my special gifts."

Student Tribute

November 12

"She always has a world of knowledge to share with us and wants us to be our very best. She's there physically and mentally all the time and she means a lot to our class."

Student Tribute

February 20

"For a teacher, if there is anything better than to be loved by a child, it is found in caring for that child and his future."

AFI Notable Quote

November 11

"She's not only a teacher but a 'guiding light' in our child's school. My daughter had problems but they were resolved because of her teacher's positive approach, which made my child feel special."

Parent Tribute

February 21

"She has a great personality and possesses caring ways which impact so favorably on her students. She organized a scrapbook containing each child's photo, favorite things, etc. to be shared with parents."

Parent Tribute

November 10

Question parents for reasons leading to poor classroom performance when others fail to make such personal contacts.

February 22

"He has an enormous talent for helping children of special needs. He buys things for them with his own money and freely gives of himself and his talents to his students."

Parent Tribute

November 9

"Her vitality allows her subjects to come alive, and her mastery of the curriculum is exceptional. The positive attitude that my child has developed is directly related to her influence."

Parent Tribute

February 23

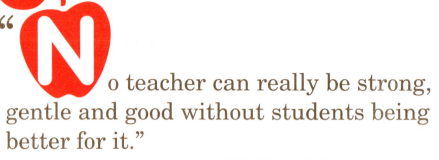

"No teacher can really be strong, gentle and good without students being better for it."

AFI Notable Quote

November 8

"My teacher's ways and special companionship helped me through some very difficult times. At graduation, she surprised me with a necklace containing a gold heart. It reflected her love and special concern for me."

Student Tribute

February 24

"She inspires children with her passion for teaching. Her environmental and science projects have awakened my son's interests and talents. She takes an active interest in his dreams."

Parent Tribute

November 7

Recognize the importance of a positive attitude in teaching when others believe that subject knowledge is enough.

February 25

"Our daughter had trouble hearing but when this teacher made adjustments and used creative approaches to testing, he brought out energies and talents we had not seen before."

Parent Tribute

November 6

"She is clearly a special teacher. She creates an involved curriculum with activities and with zest and excitement. She is nothing short of inspirational to her students. My child skips to school each day."

Parent Tribute

February 26

"Teachers whose confidence in self is strong will dare defy the doubting throng."

AFI Notable Quote

November 5

"She excels in multi-instructional techniques so that every child has some opportunity for success. Success is a key word in her classroom. It's at the core of everything she does."
Parent Tribute

February 27

"There is so much to say about this special lady! My son loves to go to school and is eager to learn. Her positive attitude rubs off on all who come in contact with her."

Parent Tribute

November 4

"He is an esteem builder! He gave me the encouragement I needed to develop a more positive attitude about myself. He made me believe in myself when others created doubts."

Student Tribute

February 28 & 29

"To me, she's the most encouraging teacher I've ever met. I give her all of my respect as a student. Everyone is equal in her class."

Student Tribute

November 3

Today, if I can put new hope within the heart of a child who has lost hope, if I can help another through any darkened hour, I shall be glad indeed.

November 2

"When my daughter said, 'I don't like school'—it became a challenge for this teacher to solve. It wasn't long after a new attitude came through and we have a happy 2nd grader!"

Parent Tribute

March 1

"My daughter lacked confidence in herself until she met this great teacher who has brought out her very best in school and out."

Parent Tribute

November 1

Talk to students in an appropriate manner and tone when others may use sarcasm or shouting.

March 2

NOVEMBER

"Each day 'happy grams' arrive home with my child. Her positive method of teaching has made such a difference. After the birth of her son, she brought him to class for a brief viewing to the kids' delight!"

Parent Tribute

March 3

"She is very structured in her presentations yet mixed with lots of enthusiasm with a 'you can do it' attitude."

Parent Tribute

October 31

"Our son was struggling in school even with average grades and because of this perceptive teacher, we discovered an eye problem. With therapy, he's doing well."

Parents' Tribute

March 4

A teacher would do nothing if he waited until he could do it so well that no one would find fault with his lesson plan.

October 30

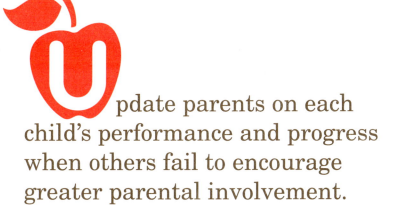

Update parents on each child's performance and progress when others fail to encourage greater parental involvement.

March 5

"Following abusiveness at home in a variety of ways, this teacher has turned my son around into a loving, positive young man. She attends his wrestling matches on Saturday!"

Parent Tribute

October 29

cat

"I have gotten good grades on all my tests because she told me I could do it. I listened to her and showed her she was right."

Student Tribute

March 6

"She is sensitive to the emotional and learning disability needs of students. Her caring and compassion come through in everything she does."

Parent Tribute

October 28

"She does not treat her LD children as special or disabled. She expects their best and provides ways for each to reach that 'best'. Their progress is exceptional."

Parent Tribute

March 7

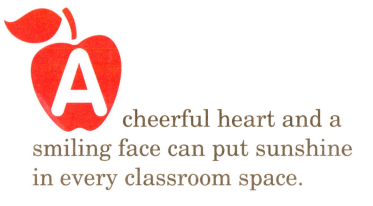 cheerful heart and a smiling face can put sunshine in every classroom space.

October 27

Value the need to share some personal time with students when others prefer group communications.

March 8

"She has made a marked difference in the life of my 11 year-old daughter. She helped her see school as a place for learning and not just a place to pass time."

Parent Tribute

October 26

"He helped and encouraged my son so
that he began to believe in himself
again. He encourages small successes."
                              Parent Tribute

March 9

"She dedicates her energies and talents to the slower child as well as the brighter ones. She inspired my daughter to where she is now in the honors program."

Parent Tribute

October 25

teacher

"She should be awarded because she helps me spell and is funny too! She's nice and is a good teacher. I trust her and she's good to us kids."

Elementary Student Tribute

March 10

"Great teachers have no limit to their endurance, no end to their faith in a child's potential for growth."

AFI Notable Quote

October 24

Wait for the best performance in each student to surface when others lack patience in adjusting to personal timetables.

March 11

"She has reversed my son's attitude and instilled in him self-confidence I never thought possible, a lifetime gift of love."

Parent Tribute

October 23

"She has had such an impact on my son that he was willing to give up playtime to go to her class! I never would have believed it in a million years: a wonderful educator."

Parent Tribute

March 12

"Thirty-two years of loving dedication to first graders can never be measured. She inspires a positive attitude in student teachers and colleagues."

Parent Tribute

October 22

"She makes learning fun and has shown special attention to my son when needed. Her positive attitude brings out the best in young children. She is an approachable, marvelous teacher."

Parent Tribute

March 13

"A child's mind, once stretched by an encouraging word and a new idea, never returns to its original capacity for growth."

AFI Notable Quote

October 21

Display a variety of student expressions and classwork when others fail to use bulletin boards creatively.

March 14

"She takes extra time to get to know something about each child and sacrifices her personal time for after-school activities."

Parent Tribute

October 20

"He's been so helpful in dealing with my son's lack of ability to pick up Spanish. He stayed after school for several hours because I was at work and helped him resolve the problem."

Parent Tribute

March 15

"She's always there to provide positive support and guidance. A gift from God to her students and her school."

Parent Tribute

October 19

"This teacher has had a great influence in my child's life, helping him through a traumatic transition. From hating school, he is achieving well and loves life again."

Parent Tribute

March 16

"Time will prove to us that payoffs from positive thinking are great. We tend to become the teachers our thoughts prepare us to be!"

AFI Notable Quote

October 18

Yield to positive alternatives in establishing classroom discipline when others rely on various forms of punishments.

March 17

"Life for my 10 year-old son had become difficult because of tragedies in his home life. This teacher began the healing process with her love and personal attention."

Parent Tribute

October 17

"My son's teacher makes a point to contact me when her day is done, to talk about his special problems. She calls me at unreasonable hours for her to meet my schedule."

Parent Tribute

March 18

"She encouraged my daughter to excel in her weak areas and does the same with each of her 32 third graders. She's extremely sensitive and caring."

Parent Tribute

October 16

"**A**s every great teacher has come to discover: as a child's confidence increases, achievement soon follows."

AFI Notable Quote

March 19

We can all pass by students
with heedless ears and careless eyes,
too bent with cares, we plod along,
deaf to the hunger in their hearts.

October 15

"She has the gift to maintain excellent discipline in her class and yet be warm and caring. Kids respond to her smiles and kind words."

Parent Tribute

March 20

"Her ability to encourage positive behavior in children is remarkable. She has made such a wonderful difference in my daughter's attitude."

Parent Tribute

October 14

Zero in on your strengths and contributions as a teacher celebrating the differences you are making with your students.

March 21

"She has given my son a completely new outlook in math. She has made him enthusiastic about her subject and his potential."

Parent Tribute

October 13

"My daughter has never responded to any teacher as she has with him. He shows great warmth, caring and respect for teenagers."

Parent Tribute

March 22

Today take the time to go on your own voyage of discovery and discover one new thing about each of your students.

October 12

"This man goes beyond the school walls and is involved in the development of children in a variety of community programs: a great role model."

Parent Tribute

March 23

"To care about every child unhesitantly and to inspire one good feeling in every student I teach everyday."

Teacher Credo

October 11

"The profession of teaching asks not how much **must** I do for my pupils, but how much **can** I do."

AFI Notable Quote

March 24

"The impact she has had on our daughter has simply been amazing. Our daughter has matured into a self-confident disciplined fourth grader. This teacher has instilled in her the importance of sticking to a task and the rewards of achieving."

Parent Tribute

October 10

"She has been a gift of excellence to our school. She commands the attention of students and goes the extra mile."

Parent Tribute

March 25

"As a first year teacher he deserves applause for sharing such an abundance of compassion and concern for my child. Doing those 'little extras' that made her feel so special, he took the time to say 'I care about you'!"

Parent Tribute

October 9

"She works with a variety of children with special needs, cares about parent opinions, and finds the time to talk out concerns. Every child feels loved."

Parent Tribute

March 26

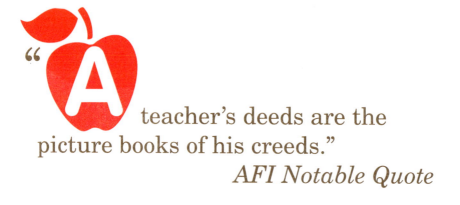

"A teacher's deeds are the picture books of his creeds."

AFI Notable Quote

October 8

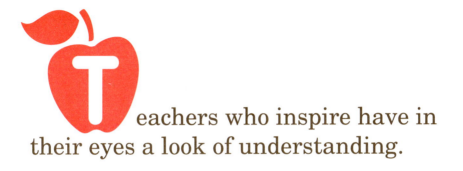

Teachers who inspire have in their eyes a look of understanding.

March 27

"As my daughter's guidance counselor, he used his instincts as a father and training as counselor to help change my daughter's future. His sensitivity, advice and many phone conferences made the difference."

Parent Tribute

October 7

"The great teacher is the one who walks into the cares of a student when the rest of the class walks out."

AFI Notable Quote

March 28

"My teacher never pressures me, never makes me feel like a failure if I can't do something right. He has a great sense of humor and is never grouchy. If he's in a bad mood he never shows it. I love going to gym class!"

Student Tribute

October 6

"His classroom is alive with teacher- and student-made maps and displays. He approaches geography, not as a single subject, but integrates it with other activities appealing to the student."

Parent Tribute

March 29

In the life of every student, there's a vacuum waiting to be filled by a teacher who can impart greater self-confidence, who can nurture undiscovered talents, and who can direct untapped energies into some form of personal fulfillment.

October 5

"She is an exceptional person as well as a teacher. She presents routine subjects as a platter of goodies which a student can devour. Our daughter has never loved school so much."

Parent Tribute

March 30

"Her love of teaching has shone through in her work. She is our prime motivator. We give our very best in and outside of the classroom. She's a friend always there to lend a helping hand."

Student Tribute

October 4

"The only teachers who are not making mistakes nor experiencing disappointments are those in retirement."

AFI Notable Quote

March 31

"If it wasn't for her, my son might still be suffering academically as well as socially. She knew how to reach him and brought out his self-confidence."

Parent Tribute

October 3

"You do what you can for someone unnamed; your motive is neither for wealth or for fame; your 'Gift of Time' goes far beyond measure, filling a storehouse in heaven with bounteous treasure."

AFI Notable Quote

October 2

"My son comes home from school with a mile-wide smile. He tells us about the fun he has had in gym class and shows us the books from the library. She has been the source of this magic."

Parent Tribute

April 1

"From the first day of school until the last, every child feels special. She constantly keeps parents informed. Her encouragement and support provides the confidence and pride in their work, memories that will last a lifetime."

Parent Tribute

October 1

She has made my son's school year a very successful and rewarding school year. She creates an atmosphere of enthusiasm for learning and instills a sense of pride in each of her students.

Parent Tribute

April 2

"The world seldom notices who the teachers are, but civilization depends on what they do and what they say."

AFI Notable Quote

April 3

"Her sensitivity, encouragement and an ongoing stream of love is what convinced and saved my child from being lost in the system. She opened doors, made phone calls to ensure my child's tests and placement."

Parent Tribute

September 30

"He has inspired me in a major way. One of the nicest people God has put on this earth. I owe him for my positive attitude, my personal value, my self-confidence."

Student Tribute

April 4

"Your sweet, tender touch on a shivering shoulder helps distressed human beings grow a little bit bolder."

AFI Notable Quote

September 29

"Despite learning that our son has a below average IQ, we discovered his good feelings about himself came from this teacher's writing class where she accented his strengths."

Parent Tribute

April 5

"I really enjoy being in her class. She makes learning fun and makes me want to be there all the time. I like the way she does projects and decorates the classroom. She takes time to attend my sports activities even on her days off."

Student Tribute

September 28

"Ultimately, students will recall the worth of their teachers not by the size of their intellects, but by the size of their hearts."

AFI Notable Quote

April 6

"After a 6-day suspension, his teacher took his own time to help him catch up and counsel him. My son now looks forward to each school day with enthusiasm."

Parent Tribute

September 27

"She has touched both of our children and has greatly contributed to their love of reading. She takes time with each and every child and works with them on an individual basis."

Parent Tribute

April 7

"Your wink of approval, an encouraging sign, helps those who've grown dimmer break into a smile."

AFI Notable Quote

September 26

"Her extra efforts in the daily school program keep these children looking forward to the next day of school. 'She never yells at us,' my grandson reminds me. 'She loves all of us'."

Grandparent Tribute

April 8

"He is a one-of-a-kind teacher. His positive and creative ways touch the lives of all he comes in contact with. His high expectations stimulate students to go for them."

Parent Tribute

September 25

"They are truly great teachers who can take us when we aren't up to par, and still appreciate us just exactly as we are."

AFI Notable Quote

April 9

"My son's band teacher has made all the difference one could imagine in changing and enriching a teenager's life for the better. He works harder in academics now as well as in music."

Parent Tribute

September 24

"She was a very inspiring person and treated you like a friend. I learned a lot from her. She never got upset with me when I kept asking her questions and needed help."

Student Tribute

April 10

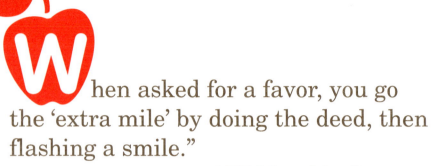

"When asked for a favor, you go the 'extra mile' by doing the deed, then flashing a smile."

AFI Notable Quote

September 23

"She adapted tests to his capability level and in turn, he was less intimidated and pressured. She has nurtured a positive influence on him and we are proud to nominate her."

Parents' Tribute

April 11

"She always finds the time to talk with parents and keeps them updated on special needs. Her encouragement and interest has made the difference in our lives."

Parent Tribute

September 22

"Great things are accomplished by teachers who, having failed, will try again. They risk their all to venture out, and having ventured, never doubt."

AFI Notable Quote

April 12

"My son hated to read but she encouraged him to see a special film with me. She encouraged him to read at night. It's been two years and we're still reading together."

Parent Tribute

September 21

"My son suffers from allergies and she has always been attentive and helpful to pick his spirits up when he isn't feeling well. She calls me and offers suggestions. She's great."

Parent Tribute

April 13

"You give of your time when nobody asks, you remember to hug the one coming in last."

AFI Notable Quote

September 20

"My daughter is a Learning Disabled Child and this teacher has given her more self confidence than in all of her schooling years. She always goes beyond the call of duty."

Parent Tribute

April 14

"This remarkable educator has had all my sons and treats each one with uncommon care and concern. She's a guiding light to all and will always go that extra mile."

Parent Tribute

September 19

"**H**appiness for a teacher lies in the joy of achievement and the thrill of creative effort with our nation's future."

AFI Notable Quote

April 15

"She didn't look as nice as she is when I first met her. But as I did my work right and acted the same, she was nice to me. What I'm trying to say is that she is a wonderful teacher."

Student Tribute

September 18

"His door is always open. He takes the time to listen and counsel. He's always ready to help with decisions which will affect the future of young people."

Student Tribute

April 16

Remember to laugh often. A good laugh can be as important to your students as a good lesson plan.

September 17

"She sends 'happy grams' home with the children and thanks parents for spending time with our children on their schoolwork. She has really changed my son and our family for the better."

Parent Tribute

April 17

"She cares deeply about her students. She establishes high expectations and helps each child attain them within their ability levels."

Parent Tribute

September 16

Happiness for a teacher lies in the joy of achievement and the thrill of creative effort with our nation's future."

April 18

"She has a pretty neat way of knowing each individual and talks to parents to make sure there isn't something she may be missing. The type of teacher we want for kids."

Parent Tribute

September 15

"Teaching is not just a job for her but a way of life. It shows in every smile she brings to a child, in every effort her students joyously make to achieve and shine before her."

Parent Tribute

April 19

"It's because of teachers who know us, those who seem to understand, that we find the going easy when we need a helping hand."

AFI Notable Quote

September 14

"My son has had low self-esteem, at least before he met this teacher. He no longer hates school or feels dumb thanks to her special ways. He has blossomed. A kind teacher was needed!"

Parent Tribute

April 20

"Great teachers build self-esteem, independence, curiosity, responsibility and character. This teacher nurtures all of these traits. Children are allowed to show initiative."

Parent Tribute

September 13

"The happiest classrooms are not ones without problems or disappointments, but ones that handle them with understanding and sensitivity."

AFI Notable Quote

April 21

"She is a model teacher with a positive attitude and great passion for her subject—plus a beautiful smile. She lavishes praise on her students and they respond with great efforts to achieve."

Parent Tribute

September 12

"She would be 'Teacher-of-the-Year' if I made the decision. My son was in a leg cast and struggling. Each week she gave him a 'buddy' to help."

Parent Tribute

April 22

The impact of a teacher's attitude toward teaching, toward students, and toward learning is profoundly more significant than any degree earned or subject mastered.

September 11

"My son loves this fourth grade teacher! She writes personal notes to me and to him regularly. She offers stickers, charts, awards and blue ribbons and they work, believe me!"

Parent Tribute

April 23

"My gym teacher became my best friend, someone I could talk with. She made a real difference in my life. I couldn't talk to any teacher—now I can talk to anyone!"

Student Tribute

September 10

"**S**trong teacher convictions that every child is gifted in some way, precede great classroom results."

AFI Notable Quote

April 24

"When so many express negatives, here was a letter from this teacher reminding us of our child's strengths. He keeps learning alive! His enthusiasm for his subject is inspiring."

Parent Tribute

September 9

"He's my daughter's teacher, motivator and friend. I never remember my daughter coming home from school so excited about Science. It's reassuring to know such teachers exist."

Parent Tribute

April 25

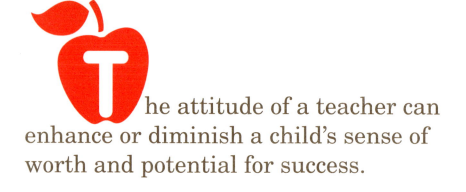

The attitude of a teacher can enhance or diminish a child's sense of worth and potential for success.

September 8

"When my son was doing poorly in Algebra, she provided the special encouragement and techniques which raised his grades and his spirits. She has left a lasting impression."

Parent Tribute

April 26

"It's a real treat to witness the passion this teacher has for her classroom tasks. She puts an extraordinary amount of time and effort into her students and their curriculum."

Parent Tribute

September 7

"Let's count our success in teaching one student at a time. Our failures in reaching some children are less significant than the ones we affect for the better."

AFI Notable Quote

April 27

"She's had a wonderful influence on my daughter. She has such a caring way of handling any situation that pops up. Her attentiveness to students is outstanding."

Parent Tribute

September 6

"She welcomes students to the computers and takes the time to help them. She helped me with the most important paper of the year and I will never forget that."

Student Tribute

April 28

"We need to celebrate excellence in teaching, with the improvement of one child at a time."

AFI Notable Quote

September 5

"He taught me that Science holds great wonders for the mind to explore. I used to hate this subject. He has a way of making us get excited about what we're doing. My favorite teacher."

Student Tribute

April 29

"He took the time to tutor my child, who has epilepsy, after school. His grades are beginning to improve. It means so much to realize that such teachers exist."

Parent Tribute

September 4

"A simple compliment may not alter a student's behavior immediately. It does help get things moving in the right direction."

April 30

"His positive attitude and enthusiasm for his subject has affected my daughter's attitude and achievement for the better. She's interested, excited and challenged for the first time."

Parent Tribute

September 3

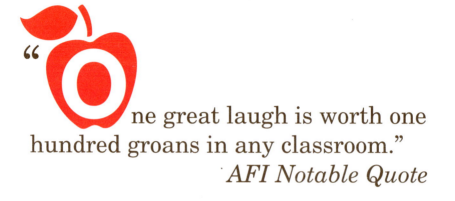

"One great laugh is worth one hundred groans in any classroom."

AFI Notable Quote

September 2

"He shows an amazing commitment to children. He arrived at 5:30 a.m. on opening day to prepare his classroom. He donates his time to a variety of after-school programs that make a difference."

Parent Tribute

May 1

"She has given my son such a positive boost to want to try harder, to achieve more. She turns his anxious, never-ending energy into an academic channel. I wish I had her secret."

Parent Tribute

September 1

$+\dfrac{1}{3}$

"She never lost her temper. She taught me maturity and good manners. Even though I didn't get the best grades, she still treated me like a gifted student."

Student Tribute

May 2

"Surely, the more we learn, the more we can do. The more we can do, the more we can learn. In all of this doing and learning, don't forget to provide your students with the most essential ingredient for learning—ENJOYMENT!"

AFI Notable Quote

May 3

"My daughter feels very comfortable with her and is able to talk about her anxieties related to her hearing disability. She arranged a pen pal with a similar disability."

Parent Tribute

August 31

"She teaches with a smile on her face, a laugh in her voice, and a heart full of love. Recently she called me during her free period and helped me resolve my son's sudden illness."

Parent Tribute

May 4

Teachers have continuous opportunities to make their commitment and their concern felt by students.

August 30

"She makes such a difference in my child's life. My son has been making such wonderful progress with her. It's hard to describe her magic. The world needs more people like her."

Parent Tribute

May 5

"His teaching approach has raised my grades from B's to A's. His funny jokes make World Cultures more interesting."

Student Tribute

August 29

"A teacher's most valuable asset is an active mind that is always finding something new, discovering and experimenting with possibilities that can make a difference in the education of a child."

AFI Notable Quote

"His personality and charisma in his work and his caring for students made my learning of math fun and easy. Never once did he raise his voice. He's interested in our future."

Student Tribute

August 28

"She is an exemplary educator who never loses sight of why she is in the profession. Her 'child-first' philosophy is evident in everything she does and says. A role model for her peers."

Parent Tribute

May 7

As a teacher, any valuable contributions you make to your students will come through the expression of your own personality. That makes you wonderfully different from the rest!

August 27

"I want to be a school teacher and she has served as a role model. She's like my mother away from home. She believes in the possibilities of every student and nurtures our best."

Student Tribute

May 8

"I nominate my algebra teacher. You can ask her the same questions over and over and she'll always show patience and understanding. She'll keep at you until you find the solution."

Student Tribute

August 26

Increasing your self-esteem as a teacher is easy. Simply continue to do good and kind things for your students and remember that you've done them.

May 9

"I'm proud to say that my son has benefited in unlimited ways from his exposure to his science teacher. On the last day of school he said, 'I hope I was a good role model.' You were!"

Parent Tribute

August 25

"I have been awed by her enthusiasm, commitment and energy. She listens, guides, and inspires in her daily activities. Thank you for your vision, for your encouragement."

Student Tribute

May 10

"We get from our students what we give them. We can find in them what we find in ourselves."

AFI Notable Quote

August 24

"These teachers made themselves available to parents and students before, after and during school. Their devotion to academics does not cloud their perception of their pupils as individuals."

Student Tribute

May 11

"She always places the needs of students above the prescribed lesson plan. She has made a special difference in advancing my child's interest in school work and in personal growth."

Parent Tribute

August 23

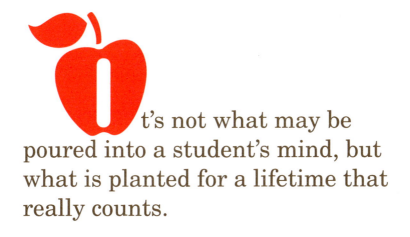

It's not what may be poured into a student's mind, but what is planted for a lifetime that really counts.

May 12

"There's only one teacher's class that remains vivid in my mind. She has taught me so much about Math and life in general. My friend, my counselor, my role model, thank you."

Student Tribute

August 22

"She provided me with her home phone number and encouraged regular contact in dealing with my son's special learning needs. She has been the stabilizing factor. Finally, results are becoming evident."

Parent Tribute

May 13

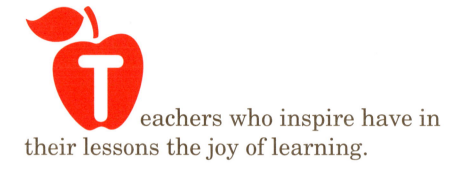

Teachers who inspire have in their lessons the joy of learning.

August 21

"She's the very essence of teaching that we need in today's schools. She's energetic, enthusiastic and eternally optimistic about her children."

Parent Tribute

May 14

"He taught me about History but also about life. He's been my 'guardian angel' and has guided me to make the right decisions, giving me self-respect and influencing my life."

Student Tribute

dog

August 20

Remind your students today that being ignorant is not as shameful as being unwilling to learn.

May 15

"I went into his Math class with a terrible attitude for that subject. By the time I got into Algebra, I loved Math because of his way of making me feel special."

Student Tribute

August 19

"Our son was frustrated and upset with schoolwork. This teacher talked out the problems on her own time with many calls between our homes. An A+ teacher!"

Parent Tribute

May 16

"**F**or a teacher to live forever in the heart and memory of even a single child is the best tribute of all."

AFI Notable Quote

August 18

"When my son had a bad reputation at school, she always believed in him. It turns out he has Attention Deficit Disorder and is settling down. It was her kindness to him when he needed it most that made the difference."

Parent Tribute

May 17

teacher

"She's special because she helps me to study Science and Social Studies. She gives treats. I hope she doesn't leave."
Elementary Student Tribute

August 17

"Building self-esteem in your students makes them take their own worth for granted, saving energy on feelings of self-doubt and using it for more productive pursuits."

AFI Notable Quote

May 18

"She is a special teacher who puts lots of effort and inspiration into the lesson plan with a helpful dose of good humor."

Parent Tribute

August 16

"If you had the chance to sit in his class as I did, you would see the rapport he has with his students. They love him. The parents love him. He has that special magic."

Parent Tribute

May 19

Perhaps a teacher's most important task in educating children is to help children learn to enjoy the process of learning.

August 15

"This teacher has a great deal of patience with kids in need of special attention. My son loves getting up for school. It's the best part of his day and he looks forward to her welcoming smile."

Parent Tribute

May 20

"She is an inspiration to all whose lives she touches...has a genuine concern for kids. My son was accused of misconduct in the cafeteria. She investigated and resolved the problem fairly."

Parent Tribute

August 14

Overly criticized children don't learn as well as those who receive a balance of praise and constructive criticism.

May 21

"He prepares and teaches exciting lesson plans for special children and takes a personal interest in their lives. They feel valued."

Parent Tribute

August 13

"She has helped me learn more in her English class than I have in all of my previous years. She has high expectations, and has opened my eyes and mind to my true potential."

Student Tribute

May 22

"The real test of a child's education is the amount of pleasure experienced in the exercise of the mind."

AFI Notable Quote

August 12

"The sincerity of her commitment to students is obvious. An example was when one student had some emotional problems and she went to visit the father at the hospital."

Parent Tribute

May 23

"She is a master teacher who has that ability to inspire learning in even the most disheartened learner. She's the cornerstone to the positive climate at her school."

Parent Tribute

August 11

"There are two ways of spreading light to your students: you can be the candle or the mirror that reflects it."

AFI Notable Quote

May 24

"She has taught me a lot about parenting. I consider her a role model. The whole world needs her to inspire greater love for our children."

Parent Tribute

August 10

"A tribute to the teacher who cared enough about my daughter to call our home when it wasn't required, to notice she works better with a desk rearranged, etc. A special person."

Parent Tribute

May 25

"Today, if I can put new hope within the heart of a child who has lost hope, if I can help another through any darkened hour, I shall be glad indeed."

AFI Notable Quote

August 9

"She makes our daughter feel special and has earned our child's love and respect. She should be proud to say 'I teach; I make a difference' and she does!"

Parent Tribute

May 26

"She moved my daughter's desk and made important adjustments for success. As she puts it, 'I wanna be a teacher like her'—she's the best."

Parent Tribute

August 8

We become our own worst enemy when we strive to be "perfect" teachers. Afraid of making mistakes or fearful of failure or ridicule, we hesitate to assert our best selves.

May 27

"When my son was having trouble paying attention in class, we worked together to coordinate home and school discipline. She understood his setbacks and arranged for him to succeed."

Parent Tribute

August 7

"My son was totally out of control early in the school year. This teacher went out of her way to make him feel special and establish controls. We're in constant contact working this problem out."

Parent Tribute

May 28

"Excellence in teaching is never an accident. It's always the result of high purpose, thoughtful planning, and persuasive ways."

AFI Notable Quote

August 6

"My thirteen-year-old had low self-esteem. She had associated problems until he met this coach who reversed his attitude and returned to him his pride."

Parent Tribute

May 29

"She devotes many, many hours preparing her lessons so that each child has some hope for success when they arrive. She sees a child, not a classroom of children, in need."

Parent Tribute

August 5

Students love to hear stories about you. Allow your students a glimpse into your life and they may allow you a glimpse into theirs.

May 30

"She has a very spirited attitude. You can tell she really enjoys her work. The 43 minutes seem to fly past because it seems more like a challenge than work. She's an inspiration."

Student Tribute

August 4

"A child's mind, once stretched by an encouraging word and a new idea, never returns to its original capacity for growth."

AFI Notable Quote

May 31

"The best compliment we can pay students is to give them the feeling that they have been set free to make their own inquiries and to come to their own conclusions."

AFI Notable Quote

August 3

"He has especially encouraged our son's imagination which can be vivid at times. Our child's self-esteem and self-confidence has grown measurably. He has never been happier at school."

Parents' Tribute

August 2

"My daughter cannot stop talking about how much she enjoys her class. She teaches life skills and shows a genuine interest in each child outside of school."

Parent Tribute

June 1

"My teacher is always there when you need her. She hardly ever yells, likes to play games with us, and loves kids!"

Elementary Student Tribute

August 1

"She is a positive force behind the warm, caring atmosphere at school. Behind the scenes, she can be found feeding a hungry child breakfast."

Parent Tribute

June 2

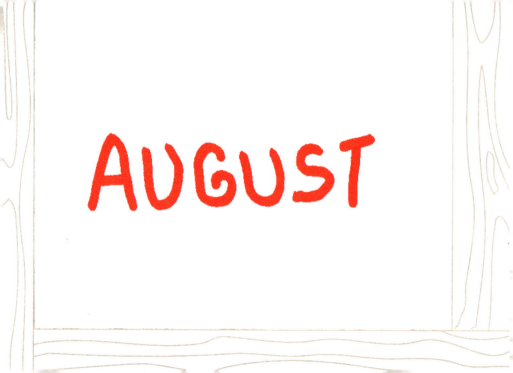

No teacher can expect to be all things to all students, not even you. When you give it your all, you can live with yourself regardless of the results.

June 3

"**L**et not your heritage to your student be texts or tests, but an unspoken treasure, the treasure of your example and caring."

AFI Notable Quote

July 31

"This teacher always greets students with good manners, kindly words, and encouragements. He also uses informality to reach students."

Parent Tribute

June 4

"She takes concerns for student needs too seriously for her own well-being. Open to new ideas, her positive attitude will be a legacy when she soon retires."

Parent Tribute

July 30

"My son was having difficulty in Math. Thanks to this teacher's positive attitude and helpful ways, he is experiencing the joy of achievement."

Parent Tribute

June 5

"Among many creative and caring gestures, this teacher has a birthday balloon flying at the desk of a happy student on their big day—summer birthdays are celebrated on designated school days."

Parent Tribute

July 29

Phone a parent this week and share something positive about his or her child. The parent's shocked and joyous reaction will make your day.

June 6

When teachers in retirement look back on their careers, the moments that stand out are the moments when they touched the life of a child in need.

July 28

"Her special way of using music with her teaching has helped my son gain an appreciation for music."

Parent Tribute

June 7

"She gave up her lunch time to work with students on projects. She stayed after school to help others. She purchased things they needed with her own money. Examples of a great teacher."

Parent Tribute

July 27

"The excellence this teacher offers should not go unnoticed in a day and age when children can feel neglected."
Parent Tribute

June 8

"When I shared my special concern about my son, she seemed to make him a 'special project'. His remarkable improvement in reading only proves how one teacher can make a world of difference."

Parent Tribute

July 26

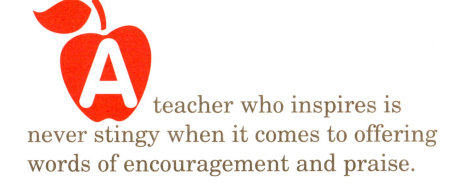

A teacher who inspires is never stingy when it comes to offering words of encouragement and praise.

June 9

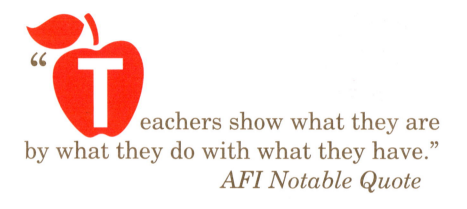

"Teachers show what they are by what they do with what they have."
AFI Notable Quote

July 25

teacher

"He makes Social Studies extra special. He is always in the hall greeting kids. He makes someone who's sad happy again. He's great."

Student Tribute

June 10

"My typing teacher showed me that a class that wasn't your favorite could still be fun. Typing has been a challenge for me, but she has made me focus and progress. Thanks."
                        Student Tribute

July 24

"She handles difficult situations wisely, putting the child's best interest first so the children enjoy learning. My daughter loves her 'next to mom'."

Parent Tribute

June 11

"He has helped me immensely over the past few months. If it wasn't for him I would not have won the District 9 Competition in drafting. His confidence in me has made the big difference."

Student Tribute

July 23

All excellence involves discipline and tenacity of purpose. This is especially true for teachers, who can feel overwhelmed, unappreciated, and fatigued in the effort to meet the needs of each learner. Remember: YOU DO MAKE A DIFFERENCE!

June 12

"**T**eachers who inspire know that in their expectations lie the possibilities for growth."

AFI Notable Quote

July 22

"It's obvious that he enjoys being a teacher and interfacing with the students. He gives generously of his time and volunteers for many community programs and goes the extra mile."

Parent Tribute

June 13

"A small but big-hearted teacher who taught me valuable lessons I can never forget: Don't be afraid to ask for help, allow people to get close to you, and be a friend to have friends."

Student Tribute

July 21

"She finds the individual strengths of students and then capitalizes on them, she is always quick to give a special award for achievement, reinforcing the positives."

Parent Tribute

June 14

"My daughter terrorized students and threw wild tantrums. No one could help or stop her except this brilliant teacher who has provided a structured environment."

Parent Tribute

July 20

"**R**eally listening to what a student has to say is the highest form of praise we can offer as teachers."

AFI Notable Quote

June 15

"Our good deeds as teachers are like stones cast into the pool of time. Though they themselves may disappear, their ripples extend to eternity."

AFI Notable Quote

July 19

"She brought love to the classroom—caring about her students individually rather than as another group to educate. We've watched our daughter grow academically and in every way."

Parent Tribute

June 16

"Her special traits of attentiveness, making available extra time and catering to my son's special needs has made him so much more excited about learning."

Parent Tribute

July 18

"My son was falling behind in Math but she rescued his downslide with patience, guidance, and 'Gifts of Time'. He adores her. She has made the difference and we would like to honor her."

Parent Tribute

June 17

"My sixth grade teacher made me feel special. She would always push me to go further. She kept me busy. She didn't put up with my wrongdoings. She showed me right from wrong."

Student Tribute

July 17

"Aim for success with your students, not perfection. Expect success with some of your students, not all. And remember that those who succeed the least, need your support the most."

AFI Notable Quote

June 18

"Many are the great teachers who have more confidence than talent, more compassion than genius."

AFI Notable Quote

July 16

"In order to be deemed 'special' you must have the capacity to put others first. You must fill a void that need immediate attention. This teacher possesses these qualities."

Parent Tribute

June 19

"This man is so devoted to his children they have him by the heart and won't let go. There is not a better behaved group of students in the school. They would not disappoint him."

Parent Tribute

July 15

"He is so full of enthusiasm for the subject and students he teaches! By sharing his zest for learning he makes all of us want to be what we want to be."

Student Tribute

June 20

"She never raises her voice and doesn't have to because everyone wants to please her. I really care about her."
Student Tribute

July 14

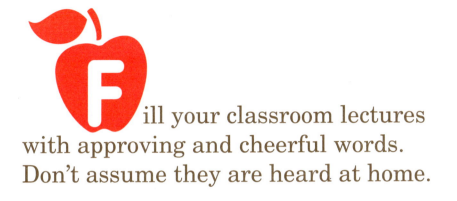

Fill your classroom lectures with approving and cheerful words. Don't assume they are heard at home.

June 21

Sometimes a caring teacher is in a better position than a caring parent to help children realize all the potential they possess and to help them believe in themselves.

July 13

"She was a very inspiring teacher and treated me more like a friend than a student. I learned so much from her. You could see she enjoyed teaching. I will remember her kindnesses."

Student Tribute

June 22

"What a dynamic, creative teacher!
She has the ability to raise and sustain
the interest of her pupils. She makes a
difference and is an inspiration to all."
Parent Tribute

July 12

"She's exceptionally attentive to students with learning problems. She's very nice and hardly ever yells at anybody! You can joke around and she'll laugh back. She is my favorite teacher."

Student Tribute

June 23

"She never fails to mail home or give to my son a positive note or card which makes him feel special. She makes many positive phone calls on her own time. She deserves praise."

Parent Tribute

July 11

"She never underscores any concern a parent may have. When my daughter missed her class photo day, she provided a shoulder to cry on and the hug my child needed most."

Parent Tribute

June 24

"The most vital teaching task is to gain a child's respect and confidence. If teachers fail in that, they cannot succeed in their instruction; for children do not learn to love a subject from teachers whom they dislike."

AFI Notable Quote

July 10

The more I meet and help celebrate teachers who have turned a child's attitude and achievement around, the more I grow in admiration of their day-to-day struggles and successes at capturing the attention and affection of students."

Dr. A.P. Witham, AFI President

June 25

"She is an action-oriented teacher who possesses large doses of creativity, compassion and competence. She challenges every child and they respond to earn her praise."

Parent Tribute

July 9

"She helped me a lot with my school work and my problems at home. She really had an influence on my life. I will never forget what she did for me. Thank you."

Student Tribute

June 26

"He's a teacher who is very positive and I can come to him anytime for help. He makes me feel he cares and listens to whatever I say with respect that I haven't found before."

Student Tribute

July 8

"Her regular communications with us on our son's ups and downs really made the difference in his school tasks. She has had a positive influence on him and we are proud to nominate her."

Parent Tribute

June 27

Caring teachers are eager to involve themselves in honest exchanges of feelings and affection with their students, hoping that one day they will graduate to being counted among their pupils' friends.

July 7

"Teaching, for all its agonies and disappointments, is still the greatest, single opportunity one has to change a child's life for the better."

AFI Notable Quote

June 28

"He was there for me when I needed help with my work. On special holidays I get him a gift because he deserves it. He's the kindest and friendliest man at school. Hope you honor him!"

Student Tribute

July 6

"He makes a difference in so many ways with us. He helps us understand when we're confused; he sees that we feel some success in whatever we're doing; he makes us believe in ourselves."

Student Tribute

June 29

"This recognition program was initiated with this teacher in mind! She never looks for recognition as she pursues each child's learning potential. Her desk is filled with parent 'Thank You' cards."

Parent Tribute

July 5

"She has made a real difference with my son. She has changed his negative attitude towards himself and made him come alive in pursuit of his special dreams."

Parent Tribute

June 30

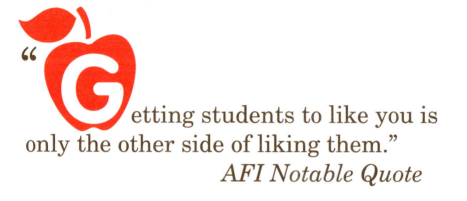

"Getting students to like you is only the other side of liking them."

AFI Notable Quote

July 4

"This year when I received an award, she was there to praise me. She always has time for me."
Student Tribute

July 3

Sometimes it's hard to smile, but work on it. To children, parents, and colleagues, a smile is a visible positive influence.

July 1

"She helped my father and me understand each other. She pushes students to strive for their best and will not slack off. She understands us."

Student Tribute

July 2

Other Calendars by Great Quotations

Apple A Day
Each Day A New Beginning
Friend Forever
Golf Forever ... Work Whenever
Home Is Where The Heart Is
Seasonings

Simple Ways To Say I Love You
To A Very Special Dad
To A Very Special Mom
Teachers Are "First Class!"

Other Books by Great Quotations

A Light Heart Lives Long
Better Place.
Food For Thought
Golden Years, Golden Words
Heal The World - Make It A
Hollywords
Reflections
Sports Page
Women on Men

Ancient Echoes
Birthday Wishes
Don't Marry, Be Happy
Great Quotes Great Comedians
Harvest Of Thoughts
Love Streams
The Best Of Business Humor
To A Very Special Husband
Who Really Said
Works of Heart

About the author...

Dr. Anthony P. Witham is the recipient of the National Award for Excellence from the Freedoms Foundation at Valley Forge. He has earned high praise from the White House, legislators, governors and school administrators for his initiatives in bringing forth the most inspiring achievements of teachers.

Dr. Witham is also the founder of the award-winning "Gift of Time" teacher tribute program. He has moderated over 300 public ceremonies of recognition to 45,000 teachers over the past 9 years. Additional information of AFI's programs can be obtained by calling (215) 269-4100 or writing AFI, Valley Forge Plaza, Suite 470, King of Prussia, PA 19406.